THE BIG PICTURE

WOMEN

WHO CHANGED THE WORLD

BY GRACE JONES

THE
SECRET
BOOK
COMPANY

THE SECRET BOOK COMPANY

©This edition was
published in 2019.
First published in 2018.

The Secret Book Company
King's Lynn
Norfolk PE30 4LS

ISBN: 978-1-912171-83-5

Written by:
Grace Jones

Edited by:
Kirsty Holmes

Designed by:
Matt Rumbelow

A catalogue record for this book
is available from the British Library.

CONTENTS

Words that look like **this** can be found in the glossary on page 30.

WOMEN WHO CHANGED THE WORLD

Throughout history, women have influenced every part of our lives. From **pioneering** scientists to powerful politicians, incredible inventors and daring explorers, women have changed the world for thousands of years.

Many women have achieved great things in their lifetimes, and it is because of them that women now have the freedoms that they once did not have. The inspirational women that you'll learn about in this book worked very hard to achieve their goals, fighting for **equality** and achieving many great things that have changed the world forever.

Not so long ago women in most countries were not allowed to vote, become doctors or scientists, or even own their own property!

Scientist

Politician

Inventor

Explorer

What did Rosa Parks do for racial equality?

How far did Amelia Earhart fly?

How did Mother Teresa heal the world?

How did Emmeline Pankhurst help get the vote for women?

How did Helen Keller overcome adversity?

How is Malala Yousafzai getting girls to school?

How did Marie Curie help us look inside the human body?

How did J.K. Rowling cast a spell over the way we read?

Is Serena Williams the most successful sportsperson in history?

How did Florence Nightingale help the sick and injured?

How did Nina Simone's music influence the world?

Let's go on a journey to find out the answers to these questions and many more about some of the greatest women who changed the world!

ROSA PARKS

Even though **slavery** had been **abolished** in 1865, in 1950s America Black people continued to be **discriminated** against in all parts of life. **Segregation** laws meant that Black Americans were not allowed to go to the same places that white Americans could, and even if they could they had to sit in different areas or rooms away from the white people.

"Of course it felt like we should all be free people and we should have the same rights as other people."
Rosa Parks

WAITING ROOM FOR COLORED ONLY.

BY ORDER
POLICE DEPT.

 Schools, restaurants and toilets are just some of the places where Black people were segregated from white people.

In 1955, a 44-year-old woman named Rosa Parks refused to give her seat to a white passenger on the bus she was travelling on in Montgomery, Alabama. She was arrested for breaking the segregation laws and taken to jail. She was eventually released but was still made to pay a fine.

Rosa Parks' act inspired other **civil rights activists** in Montgomery to **boycott** the buses. The boycott was so successful that it continued for 381 days. Eventually, some people were charged for breaking the segregation laws. When one of these cases was taken to court, a judge ruled that segregated seating on buses was **unconstitutional**.

The Civil Rights Act of 1964 made segregation in schools, public places and the workplace illegal.

At that time, 75% of people travelling on the buses in Montgomery were Black.

 The Voting Rights Act in 1965 gave all Black Americans the right to vote.

The Fair Housing Act of 1968 banned discrimination against people when they were looking to rent or buy houses.

'68

The civil rights movement ended in around 1968, by which time many laws had been passed to end segregation and achieve racial equality.

Rosa Parks is often called the 'Mother of the Civil Rights Movement' because her bus boycott started a wave of protests across America that helped to inspire the movement. The civil rights movement fought for racial equality and an end to segregation.

AMELIA EARHART

Amelia Earhart was born in the United States (US) in 1897 and, from a young age, she was interested in aeroplanes. In 1908, she saw the first people ever to fly an aeroplane, the Wright Brothers, fly at a fair near to where she lived.

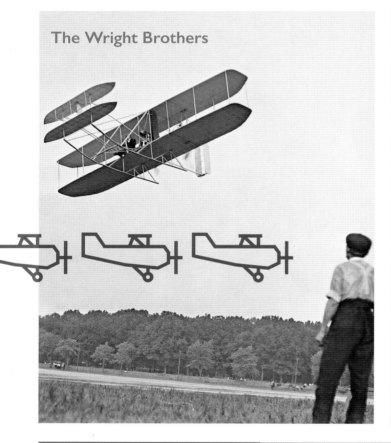

The Wright Brothers

#1 The first woman to fly to 4,267 metres.

#1 The first woman to fly at a speed of 291 kilometres per hour.

#1 The first person to fly solo from Los Angeles, US, to Mexico City, Mexico.

In 1920, Amelia visited an air show and flew as a passenger in an aeroplane. After her experience, Amelia knew that all she wanted to do was become a pilot. She worked hard to save up enough money to pay for flying lessons, and later bought her very own aeroplane.

Amelia Earhart's first aeroplane was bright yellow and called the 'Canary'.

In 1928, Amelia Earhart became the first woman to fly across the Atlantic Ocean in an aeroplane. She flew with two other male pilots. However, Amelia wanted to do this crossing alone. On the 20th of May, 1932, she made her dream a reality and she became the first ever woman to successfully fly across the Atlantic Ocean solo.

14 HOURS

OVER 3,000 KILOMETRES

The plane that she flew in was a Lockheed Vega 5B.

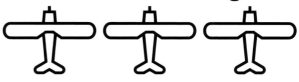

Amelia Earhart's plane took off from Newfoundland, Canada and landed in Londonderry, Northern Ireland.

Amelia Earhart became famous across the world for her daring flights and her role as an equal rights activist. Through her achievements, she inspired many other female pilots to follow in her footsteps when **aviation** was still a male-dominated world.

FIRST DAY OF ISSUE

HONORING

AMELIA EARHART

1897-1937

AMELIA EARHART'S FEATS PLACE HER AMONG THE LEGENDARIES OF AVIATION. SHE WAS THE FIRST WOMAN TO FLY THE ATLANTIC, THE FIRST WOMAN TO FLY NON-STOP ACROSS THE UNITED STATES, THE FIRST WOMAN TO FLY FROM HAWAII TO THE UNITED STATES AND THE FIRST WOMAN TO BE HONORED WITH THE DISTINGUISHED FLYING CROSS.

Art Craft

In 1937, Amelia Earhart and her navigator Fred Noonan went missing over the Pacific Ocean while attempting to fly around the world. Despite many search efforts, Earhart, Noonan and her plane were never seen again.

Earhart was awarded the Distinguished Flying Cross for her aviation achievements.

ATCHISON JUL 24 9-AM 1963 KANS.

9

MOTHER ✝ TERESA

Mother Teresa was born in 1910 in Üsküp, which is now known as Skopje, in modern-day Macedonia. She was raised as a **Catholic** from an early age and decided to devote her life to God and to helping others. When she was 18 years old she moved to India to become a **missionary** and a teacher.

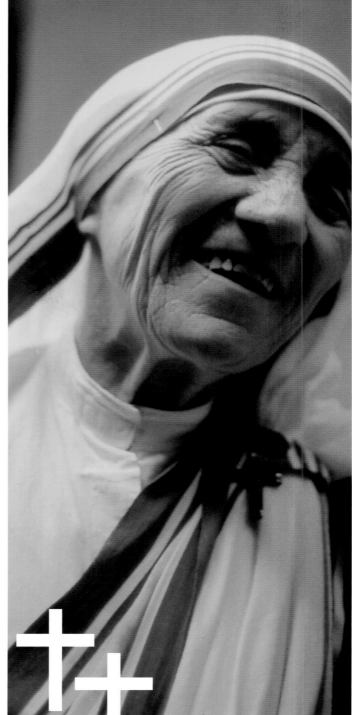

Macedonia

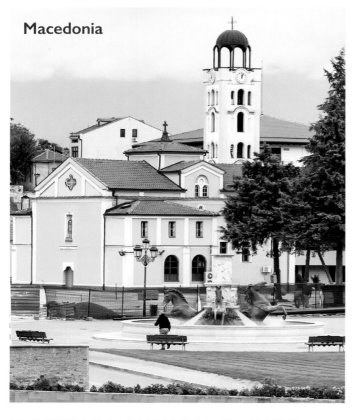

Mother Teresa saw many poor people in India and one day she felt a calling from God to help these people. In 1950, Mother Teresa started a group called the 'Missionaries of Charity' with the support of the Catholic Church to help the sick and poor. She wasn't a rich woman and sometimes had to beg for food, but she still tried to feed and help some of the poorest people in India. She visited **slums** to provide food and nursed those who were sick.

Under Mother Teresa, the charity grew and other nuns who were part of the organisation travelled to other parts of India to help people in need. Other countries started to recognise her work and began to follow her as an example of hope.

When the Missionaries of Charity first started there were only 13 members, but today the group has over 5,000 sisters and 100,000 volunteers in more than 130 countries who continue to help people all over the world.

Mother Teresa set out to change the world and she did so through her faith, her message of hope and her tireless work in caring for others. Mother Teresa and the people who helped her have saved thousands of lives around the world.

1910–1997

EMMELINE PANKHURST

In Britain before 1918, only some men had the right to vote in elections to decide who the next government should be. Emmeline Pankhurst led a group of women, known as the Suffragettes, who campaigned for women to be allowed to vote and have a say in how the country was run.

'Suffrage' is the name for the right to vote in elections. Women's suffrage means the right for women to vote.

"We are here not because we are law-breakers; we are here in our efforts to become law-makers."
Emmeline Pankhurst

At first, the Suffragettes used non-violent means of protest. Emmeline and her daughters Christabel and Sylvia were from a wealthy family, and they led and helped all women to protest against the decision not to allow women to vote. After a while, the protests became more passionate and violent, and women, including the Pankhursts, chained themselves to railings, broke shop windows and got arrested so that the government would listen to them and give women the vote.

Emmeline Pankhurst herself was arrested several times. In 1913, Emily Wilding Davison threw herself in front of the king's horse at the 1913 Derby and died four days later. When World War I broke out in 1914, Emmeline Pankhurst instructed the Suffragettes in the UK and also in the US to put their cause on hold and help. Many of these women went to work in jobs that usually only men were allowed to do in order to support the war effort.

After the war, the Suffragettes were able to persuade the Prime Minister to give the vote to some women over the age of 30, and by 1928 women were given the vote on the same terms as men. Emmeline Pankhurst supported Christabel when she ran for government, and continued campaigning for equality and women's rights.

Emmeline Pankhurst died in 1928 at the age of 69, leaving a legacy of equality behind her.

HELEN KELLER

Helen Adams Keller was born in 1880 in Alabama in the US. At 19 months old, she became ill from a mystery illness, which left her blind and deaf. As she grew up, some people thought that Keller would never be able to learn, but her mother found a teacher called Anne Sullivan to help Helen.

Helen Adams Keller   Anne Sullivan

When Anne first met Helen, she brought her a doll. She put the doll into one hand and then pressed the letters of the word D-O-L-L into her other hand. Even though Helen could learn the shape of the letters, she still did not know that the letters had any meaning to the object that she held in her other hand.

D-O-L-L

W-A-T-E-R

One day, Anne put Helen's hand under running water and wrote the letters for 'water' in her other hand. Helen realised that what the letters meant were connected to what she was feeling in her other hand: the running water. That day, Helen learnt many other words and what they meant. Finally, Anne had taught her the connection between an object and its name.

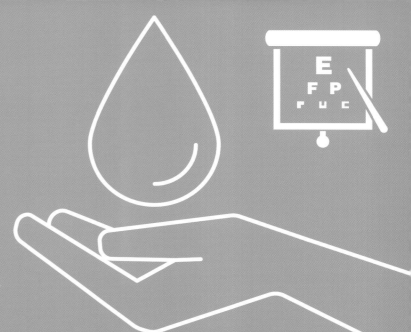

Helen Keller became the first deafblind college graduate.

Anne went on to teach Helen how to read entire books in **braille**, use a typewriter and learn to talk over the course of 20 years by feeling sound vibrations and how people moved their lips to make certain sounds.

As Helen grew older and learned more about the world around her, she wanted to help other people who were like her. She travelled around the country giving speeches and raising money for charities who helped those who were deaf and blind. She also visited injured soldiers during World War II to encourage them to not give up on her own message of hope.

Helen Keller was and still is an inspirational example of how determination, hard work and belief can allow a person to triumph over adversity no matter how many challenges they must overcome.

MALALA YOUSAFZAI

• •

Malala Yousafzai was born in the city of Mingora, Pakistan, in 1997. As she grew up, she noticed that many girls around her did not go to school, or even have the rights to any education. Her own father ran a school for girls and encouraged her to follow her ambitions to become a teacher, doctor or a politician.

"When the whole world is silent, even one voice becomes powerful."
Malala Yousafzai

What do I want to be when I grow up?

Doctor

Teacher

VOTE Politician

When Malala was around ten years old, a group called the **Taliban** began to take control of the region she lived in. The Taliban said that women should stay at home and schools for girls were shut down. Malala began to speak out about the bad things the Taliban were doing on a blog. The blog was very popular and even though Malala wrote under a fake name, the Taliban found out that she was writing it and they started to send her family death threats.

BLOG

One day in 2012, Malala was returning home from school on a bus. The bus was stopped and a member of the Taliban identified Malala and shot her. The bullet went through her head, neck and shoulder. Malala was seriously injured, and was flown to a hospital in England. However, she recovered and was back at school in England within six months.

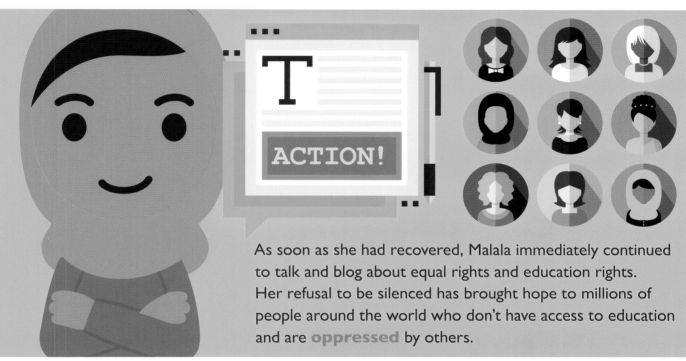

As soon as she had recovered, Malala immediately continued to talk and blog about equal rights and education rights. Her refusal to be silenced has brought hope to millions of people around the world who don't have access to education and are **oppressed** by others.

Malala Yousafzai was the youngest person to receive the Nobel Peace Prize in 2014.

MARIE CURIE

In 1896, a French scientist named Henri Becquerel discovered that an element, uranium, **emitted** energetic particles or 'active' rays. Marie Curie, a French-Polish scientist, was interested in Becquerel's discovery and wanted to find out more.

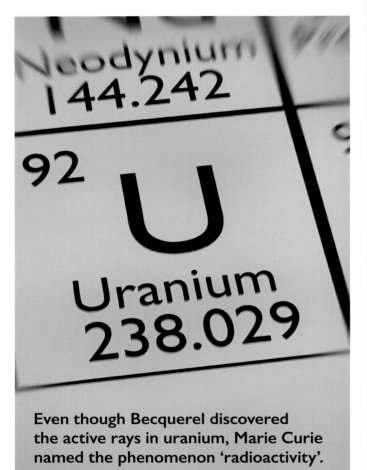

Neodynium
144.242

92 U

Uranium
238.029

Even though Becquerel discovered the active rays in uranium, Marie Curie named the phenomenon 'radioactivity'.

Marie Curie, alongside her husband Pierre Curie, began to experiment. While conducting an experiment, she noted that the material left after she had extracted the uranium seemed to be more 'active' than the uranium itself. She decided that there must be other, more active elements contained within the material. Her theory was right and Marie and Pierre discovered two new radioactive elements, polonium and radium, in 1898.

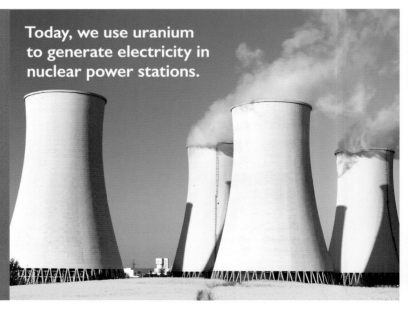

Today, we use uranium to generate electricity in nuclear power stations.

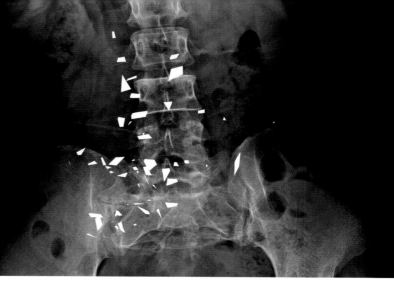

During the rest of her life, Curie worked on researching the uses and properties of radium. She also helped to save millions of lives in World War I by developing **portable** x-ray machines that could locate the positions of **shrapnel** in soldiers' bodies, which doctors could then identify and remove. She died in 1934 of a disease called aplastic anaemia, probably due to her exposure to radiation for many years.

Marie Curie was the first woman to win the Nobel Prize and the first person to win the Nobel Prize twice. The second was awarded in 1911 for her later discoveries of radium and polonium.

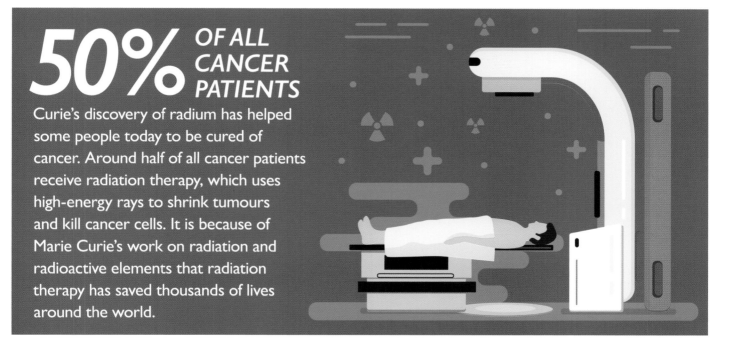

50% OF ALL CANCER PATIENTS

Curie's discovery of radium has helped some people today to be cured of cancer. Around half of all cancer patients receive radiation therapy, which uses high-energy rays to shrink tumours and kill cancer cells. It is because of Marie Curie's work on radiation and radioactive elements that radiation therapy has saved thousands of lives around the world.

J.K. ROWLING

One day in 1990, a woman called Joanne Rowling was travelling on a train from Manchester to London. On that journey, she thought of an idea for a book. It was about a young wizard who lived in a magical world. After the journey, she put pen to paper and started to write the book.

After years of writing, Rowling finished her first book. At that time, she was living in Scotland and was struggling to support herself and her daughter. She took her book to many **publishers** who rejected it, until one editor, Barry Cunningham, agreed to publish it. That book was called Harry Potter and the Philosopher's Stone.

In 1997, Rowling's first book was published and won many prestigious book awards. She went on to write many more books that were part of the Harry Potter series and achieved world-wide fame.

80 LANGUAGES

Translated into
68 languages

400m

Over 400 million books sold

3m

In the US,
Harry Potter
and the
Prisoner
of Azkaban
sold over
3 million
copies in
its first
48 hours.

11m

Harry Potter
and the Deathly
Hallows sold
11 million
copies in
the first
24 hours
of its
release.

The Harry Potter series has now been made into hugely successful films starring the actors Daniel Radcliffe, Emma Watson and Rupert Grint as Harry Potter, Hermione Granger and Ron Weasley. The Harry Potter books, films and **merchandise** are estimated to be worth tens of billions of pounds and have made J.K. Rowling hundreds of millions of pounds.

J.K. Rowling is involved with many charities and in 2011 alone she donated over 120 million pounds. She is also considered by many to be the most influential writer in the world.

The Harry Potter books sparked an interest in reading for children at a time when the number of children reading was decreasing. She also captivated children and adults alike with the magic of her writing and the fantastical world that she has created.

SERENA WILLIAMS

Serena Jameka Williams was born in Michigan in the US in 1981 and is the youngest of five sisters. Serena started playing tennis at the age of three with her elder sister Venus. At just four years old she had won her first tournament. In their early years, Serena and Venus were coached by their father Richard Williams.

Serena Williams, Venus Williams

As the girls improved, Richard moved the family to Florida so that they could train under professional coaches. In 1995, Serena began to compete in professional adult tournaments and two years later she was ranked at number 99 in the world. In 1999, at the age of just 17, she beat her sister in the final of the US Open and won her first Grand Slam title.

Serena went from strength to strength and has won over 72 singles titles and 23 doubles titles with her sister Venus. This includes 23 Grand Slam titles, which has made her the most successful tennis player ever.

Serena often played against her sister Venus in tournaments.

319 weeks ranked as world no. 1

4 Olympic gold medals

Over 84 million dollars in prize money

23 Grand Slam singles titles

Serena Williams is the most successful tennis player in history. Serena and her sister Venus have inspired children, especially girls, to pick up a tennis racket and start playing tennis. Serena has also been a strong and outspoken supporter of equal rights.

"If no one believes in her it does not matter. She believes in herself. Nothing stops her. No one can touch her. She is woman." An extract taken from Serena Williams' poem 'She is Woman'.

FLORENCE NIGHTINGALE

Florence Nightingale was born in 1820 in Italy to British parents. From an early age, Florence helped to look after the sick and poor people near to where her family lived. As she grew older, she believed that nursing was her **divine calling** and so she began her training in 1850. After finishing, she worked in several hospitals and was quickly recognised for her impressive work in improving **hygiene** practices and saving lives.

Florence Nightingale was named after the city she was born in – Florence, Italy.

In 1854, the British Secretary of State for War requested that Nightingale organise a group of nurses to look after the sick and injured causalities from the Crimean War. When Nightingale arrived, she was shocked by the filthy and unhygienic conditions that she found there. There were patients lying in their own **excrement**, rodents running around and the hospital lacked basic medical supplies, such as bandages.

More soldiers were dying from diseases than from their battle injuries.

Nightingale ordered for the hospital to be cleaned from top to bottom. Nightingale, the other nurses and the least sick patients helped to make and keep the hospital clean. In the evenings, Nightingale would visit each patient carrying a lamp and so the soldiers nicknamed her the 'Lady with the Lamp'. Through her hard work, **compassion** and dedication to improving the hygiene and care conditions at the hospital she reduced the death rate by over two-thirds.

As well as 'Lady with the Lamp', Nightingale was also known as the 'Angel of Crimea'.

St. Thomas' Hospital

The Crimean War began in 1853 between the countries of Britain, France, Turkey and Sardinia against the Russian Empire.

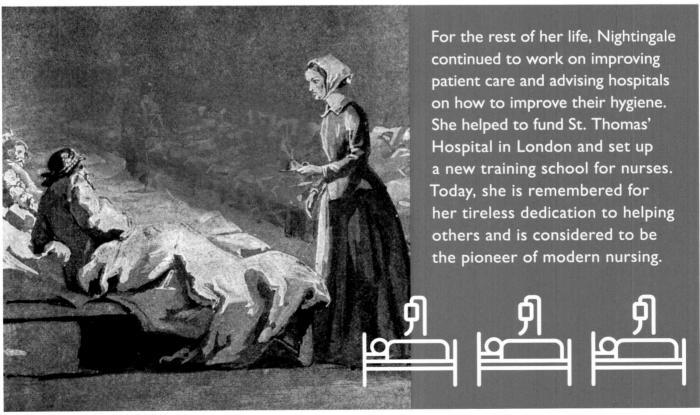

For the rest of her life, Nightingale continued to work on improving patient care and advising hospitals on how to improve their hygiene. She helped to fund St. Thomas' Hospital in London and set up a new training school for nurses. Today, she is remembered for her tireless dedication to helping others and is considered to be the pioneer of modern nursing.

NINA SIMONE

Eunice Kathleen Waymon, now known as Nina Simone, was born in North Carolina in the US to a poor family. She started to learn how to play the piano at the age of three. She decided she wanted to be a pianist and her music teacher helped to pay for her musical education. When she was older she had to drop out of one music school because she did not have enough money and was rejected from another.

When she started to play in Atlantic City, she took the stage name 'Nina Simone'.

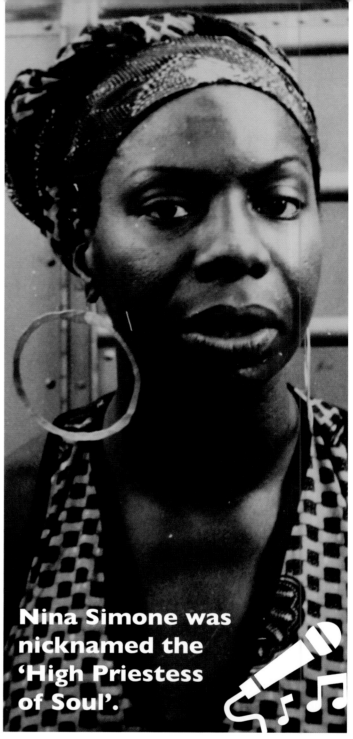

Nina Simone was nicknamed the 'High Priestess of Soul'.

In the 1950s, without money and unable to study music, she started playing piano and singing in jazz and blues clubs in Atlantic City. Simone gained popularity over the years and signed a record deal. She released her first album in 1958. Nina Simone went on to produce many albums that covered many different genres including, jazz, blues, folk and classical music.

In the 1960s, Simone became the musical voice of the civil rights movement. Many of her songs were about racial discrimination and the problems Black Americans faced within society. As well as writing music, Simone was an active civil rights protester too.

Nina Simone struggled with mental illness, especially in her later life and was eventually diagnosed with **bipolar disorder** in the 1980s.

Nina Simone inspired a whole generation of musicians that followed including The Beatles, Elton John, Madonna and Beyoncé to name just a few. Her work continues to inspire people and musicians alike. She also leaves a strong legacy in the world of political activism and the fight for equal rights.

TIMELINE: WOMEN WHO CHANGED THE WORLD

1854: Florence Nightingale travelled with other nurses to help those injured in the Crimean War.

1887: Helen Keller learns the word 'water' and connects the material to the word.

1928: Amelia Earhart becomes the first woman to cross the Atlantic Ocean solo in an aeroplane.

1958: Nina Simone releases her first album, Little Girl Blue.

1955: Rosa Parks refuses to give her seat to a white passenger on the bus she was travelling on in Montgomery, Alabama.

1950: Mother Teresa starts the 'Missionaries of Charity' with the support of the Catholic Church to help those who needed it.

1997: J.K. Rowling publishes her first book, Harry Potter and the Philosopher's Stone.

1999: Serena Williams wins her first Grand Slam title at the US Open at the age of 17.

2012: Malala Yousafzai is shot on a school bus by a member of the Taliban.

MORE WOMEN WHO CHANGED THE WORLD

Anne Frank – Young girl who kept a diary while hiding from the Nazis; one of the most-most widely read books in the world.

Hilary Rodham Clinton – Former First Lady of the United States, then Secretary of State. Was the first female democrat to run for president in 2016.

Ada Lovelace – Wrote the first computer **algorithm** and predicted that computers would do more than maths in the 1800s.

Sacagawea – Native American woman who helped build relations between settlers and the Native American people.

Jocelyn Bell Burnell – Discovered the first **radio pulsars**.

Elizabeth Freeman – First Black slave to file for her freedom and win, effectively ending slavery in Massachusetts.

There are lots more women who, throughout history, have made big decisions, invented or discovered important things, and campaigned for change. Without them, the world would not be the same. Who else can you think of? Which women have made the biggest impact on your world?

GLOSSARY

abolished
to have put an end to something, usually a system, practice or institution

adversity
a difficult or unfortunate situation

algorithm
a list of instructions computers follow in order to solve a problem

aviation
to do with the design, production or flying of aircraft

bipolar disorder
a mental disorder that causes unusual changes in mood, energy and activity levels

boycott
to stop using the goods or services of a certain company or country as a means of protest

braille
a system of writing and printing which uses a combination of dots and points to represent letters and allows people who are blind to read by touch

Catholic
relating to the Roman Catholic faith, which is a branch of Christianity

civil rights activists
people who are part of a political movement to secure equal opportunities and rights

compassion
a feeling of deep sympathy for another who is suffering, along with a strong desire to stop that suffering

discriminated
to have treated people unjustly for reasons, such as their race, gender, sex or age

divine calling
a calling from God to do something

emitted
to have sent out

equality
the state of being equal, especially in rights, status and opportunity

excrement
a type of human waste, often called poo

Grand Slam
the four most important yearly tennis events

hygiene
the conditions or practices that keep a person or a place clean

merchandise
objects that are bought and sold

missionary
a person sent by the church to carry out charitable work in, for example, a school or hospital

oppressed
to have put cruel or unjust restrictions upon a person through the use of authority and power

pioneering
involving new ideas that are usually first in a field of progress

portable
easily carried or moved by hand

publishers
a person or company whose business is
to publish books or printed materials

racial
relating to race

radio pulsars
very dense, spinning objects in space which
emit beams of radio waves

segregation
the act of separating or setting apart people
into groups

shrapnel
small pieces of metal that come from
exploded bombs, mines or shells

slavery
the practice of being a slave or owning slaves

slums
heavily populated and run-down parts of cities
that poor people live in

Taliban
an Islamic extremist political and military
organisation in Afghanistan and Pakistan

unconstitutional
if something goes against the principles that
govern a country

INDEX